Fact Finders™

Energy at Work

Wind Power

by Josepha Sherman

Consultant:
Steve Brick, Associate Director
Energy Center of Wisconsin
Madison, Wisconsin

Mankato, Minnesota

Fact Finders is published by Capstone Press
151 Good Counsel Drive, P.O. Box 669, Mankato, Minnesota 56002
www.capstonepress.com

Library of Congress Cataloging-in-Publication Data
Sherman, Josepha.
    Wind power / by Josepha Sherman.
        p. cm.—(Fact finders. Energy at work)
    Includes bibliographical references and index.
    ISBN 0-7368-2475-8 (hardcover)
    Contents: Windsurfing—Wind—Wind power history—Generating electricity—Benefits and drawbacks—The future—Making a pinwheel.
        1. Wind power—Juvenile literature. I. Title. II. Series.
TJ825.S455 2004
333.9'2—dc22   2003015941

Editorial Credits
Gillia Olson, editor; Juliette Peters, designer; Alta Schaffer, photo researcher; Eric Kudalis, product planning editor

Photo Credits
Cover: Wind turbine in Hawaii, Corbis/Royalty Free

Corbis/Douglas Peebles, 21; Greg Smith, 14; H. Armstrong Roberts, 12; Kevin Schafer, 25; Mark Gamba, 6–7; ML Sinibaldi, 16–17; Royalty Free, 1, 26–27; Terry W. Eggers, 23; Warren Morgan, 4–5
Corbis Sygma/Amet Jean Pierre, 19
Copy of an original in the Dept. of Special Collections, Case Western Reserve University Library, Cleveland, Ohio, 10
Getty Images/Hulton Archive, 8–9
The Image Finders/Mark E. Gibson, 24
John Elk III, 15
Jon Gnass/Gnass Photo Images, 13
NREL/Northern Power Systems, 22
Rutland Historical Society, 11

1 2 3 4 5 6 09 08 07 06 05 04

Table of Contents

Chapter 1

Windsurfing

High winds blow down the Columbia River Valley between Washington and Oregon. They are funneled between the high cliffs of the Columbia River Gorge.

A man climbs on what looks like a surfboard with a sail. As he pulls up the sail, it catches the wind. He cuts through the water. At the top of a wave, he bends the sail. The board leaves the water's surface, and he is airborne.

Windsurfers use their sails to catch the wind in just the right way to glide, jump, and flip on the water. It is just one way to use the power of wind.

A windsurfer catches the wind in the Columbia River Gorge.

Chapter 2

Wind

Wind occurs as hot air rises and cool air moves in to take its place. The Sun makes this process possible by heating the air unevenly. When the hot air rises high enough, it cools down again and falls toward the ground. The moving air creates a spinning effect. We feel this spinning air as wind.

Visitors to an ocean beach can feel a good example of uneven heating. Sand heats up surrounding air faster than water. During the day, air above the beach heats up and rises. Cool sea air rushes inland to take the warm air's place. Almost always, cool ocean breezes blow on the coasts.

People fly kites in the swift breezes on the coast.

Chapter 3

Wind Power History

People first used wind power to push sailboats. Sails have been used for thousands of years.

It is possible that windmills were used almost 4,000 years ago to pump water. Historians do know that around A.D. 600, the Persians of present-day Iran used windmills. People there used windmills to grind their grain into flour.

About 500 years later, Europeans began using windmills. They also used windmills to grind grain.

In the 1500s, European farmers used windmills to grind their grain, as shown in this print by Stradanus.

▲ Brush's wind turbine was much larger than the man cutting the lawn below it (right).

Electricity

In the late 1800s, electric lights and machines became available. People without electric service soon used wind machines to make electricity for lights and radios. In 1888, Charles F. Brush was the first person to use a large wind **turbine** to make electricity. His wind turbine made enough electricity for about 10 homes.

In 1931, Russia built the first commercial power plant that used a wind turbine to make electricity. The Russian machine made 100 **kilowatts** of electricity.

By 1941, a Vermont company had made a 1,250-kilowatt wind turbine. Laid end to end, the two blades measured 175 feet (53 meters). The turbine worked until 1945, when one of the blades broke off.

FACT!

The blades of several large wind turbines built in the 1940s broke off while in use. Scientists learned from these events. They built turbines out of better materials.

The two blades of the Vermont wind turbine measured 175 feet (53 meters). ➡

Fossil Fuels

People continued to experiment with wind power, but it was not widely used after World War II (1939–1945). Instead, people used more fossil fuels, such as oil and coal. Fossil fuels were cheaper and more reliable than wind power.

▲ In the 1950s, many people used coal to heat homes. Companies delivered coal to their houses.

Then, in the 1970s, oil prices rose. People wanted to find cheaper ways to get energy. They made wind turbines stronger and more lightweight.

People placed tens or hundreds of these improved wind turbines together to create **wind farms**. In 1981, a wind farm at Altamont Pass in California was built. It now has more than 7,000 machines.

The wind farm at Altamont Pass was the first large wind farm in the ▼ United States.

13

▲ A worker steadies part of a wind machine as it is lifted into place. The construction of wind machines has greatly increased in recent years.

FACT!

California, Texas, Iowa, and Minnesota, in that order, make the most wind power in the United States.

Wind Power Today

Today, wind power is the fastest-growing **renewable energy** source. The number of new wind machines in the United States increased 25 percent from 1997 to 2001. In 2002, the increase was even higher. Still, wind power makes up only 1 percent of the energy used in the United States.

Some countries in Europe use much more. Denmark gets 20 percent of its electricity from wind power.

Denmark uses wind machines across the country to generate 20 percent of its power. ➡

Chapter 4

Generating Electricity

People still use sails to move boats. Some farms still use windmills to pump water for livestock and to irrigate crops. To create electricity, people use wind turbines.

Most wind turbines look like giant fans. They can stand up to 200 feet (61 meters) tall. The steel or concrete towers are strong enough to hold up the rest of the turbine.

Wind turbines are shaped like giant fans.

Every wind turbine has at least one blade. Most have three blades. Blades on large turbines are between 50 and 80 feet (15 and 24 meters) long.

To spin, the blades use the same forces that allow planes to fly. Wind creates a pocket of low pressure just downwind of the blade. The blade is pulled toward that low pressure. This process is called lift.

The blades are specially shaped to make air move faster on one side than the other, creating lift and making ▼ the blade turn.

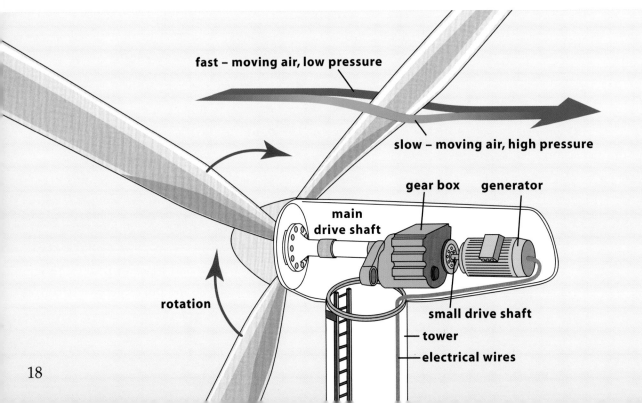

fast – moving air, low pressure

slow – moving air, high pressure

gear box   generator

main
drive shaft

rotation

small drive shaft

tower

electrical wires

Generating Electricity

The blades are attached to a rod called the main **drive shaft**. Usually, the drive shaft turns a series of gears. Each gear turns faster than the last. The last gear turns a small drive shaft very fast. This rod powers the **generator**. The generator makes electricity.

Wind needs to blow above certain speeds to turn the blades of a turbine. Smaller turbines need wind speeds greater than 9 miles (14 kilometers) per hour. Larger turbines need wind speeds greater than 12 miles (19 kilometers) per hour.

▲ The gears and generator of a turbine are in a compartment large enough that people can walk around inside.

F A C T !

If two of the blades of the largest wind turbine today were placed end to end, they would stretch farther than the length of a football field.

Chapter 5

Benefits and Drawbacks

Wherever the wind blows strong enough, people can harness wind energy. But many things must be considered before building a wind turbine. As with any source of energy, wind power has benefits and drawbacks.

Benefits

Wind is a clean source of energy. Wind turbines do not give off **pollution**. Fossil fuels, like oil and coal, cause pollution when burned to make energy.

Wind turbines create electricity for Hawaii.

Wind power helps keep energy costs stable. Once a turbine is built, the wind itself is free. Fossil fuel prices can increase, driving up the cost of making energy. Using more wind power will keep changes in fossil fuel prices from raising the overall cost of energy. The price of energy will not vary as much.

▲ A wind turbine added to a diesel generator system helps reduce the amount of diesel gasoline needed at this site in Antarctica.

Wind turbines take up little ground area. Often, farmers build wind turbines in fields and pastures. They can continue to graze their livestock and plant crops around the towers.

Drawbacks

Wind turbines can be noisy. Engineers have worked to make wind turbines quieter. Most modern wind turbines are not noisy. People also build them away from homes or businesses to keep noise from bothering people.

Because wind turbines take up little room, livestock can still graze in the fields. ➡

Wind does not blow at the same speed all the time. To keep a steady power supply, people need to store power in batteries or have a backup power supply.

Some people think wind turbines are ugly and spoil countryside views. Wind turbines cannot be hidden. They must be high enough to catch the wind.

Some people believe that wind turbines can spoil the view of the landscape.

Wind turbines can hurt birds. Some birds fly into turbine blades. People try to build wind farms away from bird migration areas. They also use turbine tower styles that stop birds from nesting there.

FACT!

"Dead calm" is a term used to describe periods of no wind.

Early turbines with open towers allowed birds to nest on them. New towers are designed to be unsuitable nesting sites for birds. ▶

Chapter 6

The Future

Engineers keep building better wind turbines. They are making turbines out of stronger, more lightweight materials. As a result, wind machines are becoming more **efficient**.

Several European countries have already built turbines in ocean waters. Winds are usually stronger and more dependable in oceans than on land. The turbines also provide needed power to crowded coastal areas without taking land space. The United States and other countries in Europe have planned future ocean turbine sites.

Turbines built in the ocean may become more common.

As today's fastest-growing energy source, wind energy is sure to be important in the future. Use of wind will increase as more people value renewable energy.

Fast Facts

- As hot air rises, cool air moves in to take its place. We feel it as wind.

- Windmills were used at least 1,400 years ago.

- In the 1880s, windmills became popular for creating electricity in areas that did not get electric service.

- California's famous Altamont Pass wind farm was started in 1981. It now has more than 7,000 turbines.

- Wind power is the fastest growing renewable energy source in the United States, but it still makes up less than 1 percent of energy used.

- Large wind turbines can be 200 feet (61 meters) tall. Blades can be between 50 and 80 feet (15 and 24 meters) long.

- In the future, people may see more turbines built in ocean waters.

Hands On: Make a Pinwheel

What You Need

ruler

piece of construction paper

scissors

thumbtack

pencil with eraser

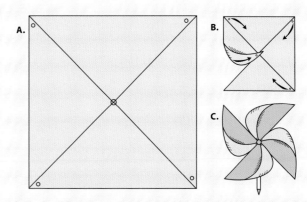

What You Do

1. With the ruler, measure an 8-inch by 8-inch (20-centimeter by 20-centimeter) square of paper. Cut out the square.

2. With the ruler, draw two diagonal lines across the square, from corner to corner.

3. Make holes with the thumbtack as shown in diagram A.

4. Carefully cut along the lines, stopping about 2 inches (5 centimeters) from the center of the square.

5. Bend each corner in toward the center in a curve until you are holding all four corners together.

6. Carefully push the thumbtack through all four corner holes.

7. Carefully push the thumbtack into the side of the pencil eraser. Let the wind turn the blades!

Glossary

drive shaft (DRIVE SHAFT)—the rod turned by a wind turbine's blades

efficient (uh-FISH-uhnt)—the quality of not wasting time or energy

generator (JEN-uh-ray-tur)—a machine that makes electricity by turning a magnet inside a coil of wire

kilowatt (KIL-uh-waht)—a unit for measuring electrical power; one kilowatt is the rate at which about 100 homes use power.

pollution (puh-LOO-shuhn)—harmful materials that dirty or damage air, water, and soil

renewable energy (ri-NOO-uh-buhl EN-er-jee)—power from sources that will not be used up, such as wind, water, and the Sun

turbine (TUR-bine)—an engine powered by water, steam, or gas moving through the blades of a fan; air is a gas that moves through the blades of a wind turbine.

wind farm (WIND FARM)—a group of wind turbines

Internet Sites

FactHound offers a safe, fun way to find Internet sites related to this book. All of the sites on FactHound have been researched by our staff.

Here's how:

1. Visit *www.facthound.com*
2. Type in this special code **0736824758** for age-appropriate sites. Or enter a search word related to this book for a more general search.
3. Click on the **Fetch It** button.

FactHound will fetch the best sites for you!

Read More

Graham, Ian. *Wind Power.* Energy Forever? Austin, Texas: Raintree Steck-Vaughn, 1999.

Snedden, Robert. *Energy Alternatives.* Essential Energy. Chicago: Heinemann Library, 2002.

Tecco, Betsy Dru. *Wind Power of the Future: New Ways of Turning Wind into Energy.* Library of Future Energy. New York: Rosen, 2003.

Index